LONDON COLLEGE OF MUSIC

Grade Seven

Classical Guitar Playing

Compiled by
Tony Skinner, Raymond Burley and Amanda Cook
on behalf of

Registry of Guitar Tutors

Printed and bound in Great Britain

A CIP record for this publication is available from the British Library
ISBN: 978-1-905908-17-2

Published by Registry Publications

Registry Mews, Wilton Rd, Bexhill, Sussex, TN40 1HY

Cover artwork by Danielle Croft. Design by JAK Images.
Music engraving by Alan J Brown, Chaz Hart and Steve Marsh.

Compiled for **LCM Exams** by

www.RegistryOfGuitarTutors.com

INTRODUCTION _____

This publication is part of a progressive series of ten handbooks, primarily intended for candidates considering taking the London College Of Music examinations in classical guitar playing. However, given each handbook's wide content of musical repertoire and associated educational material, the series provides a solid foundation of musical education for any classical guitar student – whether intending to take an examination or not. Whilst the handbooks can be used for independent study, they are ideally intended as a supplement to individual or group tuition.

Examination entry

An examination entry form is provided at the rear of each handbook. This is the only valid entry form for the London College Of Music classical guitar examinations.

Please note that *if the entry form is detached and lost, it will not be replaced under any circumstances and the candidate will be required to obtain a replacement handbook to obtain another entry form.*

Editorial information

Examination performances must be from this handbook edition. All performance pieces should be played in full, including all repeats shown; the pieces have been edited specifically for examination use, with all non-required repeat markings omitted. Tempos, fingering and dynamic markings are for general guidance only and need not be rigidly adhered to, providing an effective musical result is achieved. In some pieces such markings are kept to a minimum to allow candidates to display individual interpretation; the omission of editorial dynamic markings does not in any way imply that dynamic variation should be absent from a performance.

Pick-hand fingering is normally shown on the stem side of the notes:
p = thumb; *i* = index finger; *m* = middle finger; *a* = third finger.

Fret-hand fingering is shown with the numbers **1 2 3 4**, normally to the left of the notehead.
0 indicates an open string.

String numbers are shown in a circle, normally below the note. For example, ⑥ = 6th string.

Finger-shifts are indicated by a small horizontal dash before the left-hand finger number.

For example, **2** followed by **-2** indicates that the 2nd finger can stay on the same string but move to another fret as a *guido finger*. The finger-shift sign should not be confused with a *slide* or *glissando* (where a longer dash joins two noteheads).

Slurs are indicated by a curved line between two notes of differing pitch. These should not be confused with *ties* (where two notes of the same pitch are joined by a curved line in order to increase the duration of the first note).

Full barrés (covering 5 or 6 strings with the first finger) are shown by a capital B, followed by a Roman numeral to indicate the fret position of the barré. *Half barrés* (covering 2 to 4 strings) are shown like this: ½B, followed by a Roman numeral to indicate the fret position of the half barré. For example, ½BI indicates a half barré at the first fret. A dotted line will indicate the duration for which the barré should be held.

Harmonics are shown with a diamond-shaped notehead. The fret at which they are to be played will be shown above each note, e.g. H12 for 12th fret, and the string number will be shown. On the stave, harmonics are generally placed at the pitch of the fretted note above which they are played – rather than the pitch at which they sound.

Arpeggiated chords, that are rolled or strummed, are indicated by a vertical wavy line to the left of the chord.

TECHNICAL WORK

 maximum of 15 marks may be awarded in this section of the examination. The examiner may ask the candidate to play *from memory* any of the scales, arpeggios or chords shown on the following pages.

The following two octave scales may be requested in *any* key: chromatic, major, harmonic and melodic minor. These are shown overleaf with 'transpositional' patterns, i.e. they can be transposed to other pitches by using the same finger pattern starting from a different fret:

- Where a transpositional pattern is written in C it can be transposed along the fifth string by starting on the following frets: 4th fret for C♯/D♭, 5th fret for D, 6th fret for D♯/E♭, 7th fret for E, 8th fret for F, 9th fret for F♯/G♭.

- Where a transpositional pattern is written in G it can be transposed along the sixth string by starting on the following frets: 4th fret for G♯/A♭, 5th fret for A, 6th fret for A♯/B♭, 7th fret for B.

Scales and arpeggios should be played *ascending and descending*, i.e. from the lowest note to the highest and back again, without a pause and without repeating the top note. It is recommended that arpeggios and double-stopped scales are played *tirando* (i.e. using free strokes) and that all other scales are played *apoyando* (i.e. using rest strokes), although tirando can be used providing a good tone is produced. Any effective and systematic combination of alternating fingers may be used to pick the strings.

Chords should be played *ascending only*, and sounded string by string, starting with the lowest root note. To achieve a legato sound, the whole chord shape should be placed on the fingerboard before, and kept on during, playing. Chords should always be played tirando, i.e. using free strokes. The following right-hand fingering is recommended for chords: *p* for all bass strings, *ima* for the treble strings.

To allow for flexibility in teaching and playing approaches, all the fingering suggestions within this handbook are not compulsory and alternative systematic fingerings, that are musically effective, will be accepted. Scales that are required in more than one fingerboard position should all be played in the same octave.

Recommended tempo	
Scales:	144 minim beats per minute
Double-stopped scales:	72 minim beats per minute
Arpeggios:	104 minim beats per minute
Chords:	132 minim beats per minute

Suggested tempos are for general guidance only. Slightly slower or faster performances will be acceptable, providing that the tempo is maintained evenly throughout.

Key Study

The Key Study links the introduction of a new key to the performance of a short melodic theme from a piece by a well-known composer. The purpose is to make the learning of scales relevant to practical music-making and therefore memorable, as well as providing the opportunity to play music outside the standard guitar repertoire.

The examiner may request you to play any, or all, of the scales within the Key Study. The examiner will also ask for a performance of ONE of the melodic themes of your choice.

Tempo markings and fingering are for guidance only and need not be rigidly adhered to, providing a good musical performance is produced. The examiner will be listening, and awarding marks, for evidence of melodic phrasing and shaping, as well as for accuracy and clarity.

The Key Study must be played entirely from memory.

C Chromatic scale - 2 octaves (Transpositional pattern)

G Chromatic scale - 2 octaves (Transpositional pattern)

C Major scale - 2 octaves (Transpositional pattern)

G Major scale - 2 octaves (Transpositional pattern)

C Harmonic Minor scale - 2 octaves (Transpositional pattern)

G Harmonic Minor scale - 2 octaves (Transpositional pattern)

C Melodic Minor scale - 2 octaves (Transpositional pattern)

G Melodic Minor scale - 2 octaves (Transpositional pattern)

G Chromatic scale - 3 octaves

G Major scale - 3 octaves

G Harmonic Minor scale - 3 octaves

G Melodic Minor scale - 3 octaves

E Harmonic Minor scale - 1 octave: 3 different fingerboard positions

6

A Major scale - 1 octave in 3rds

A Major scale - 1 octave in 6ths

A Major scale - 1 octave in 8ths

A Major scale - 1 octave in 10ths

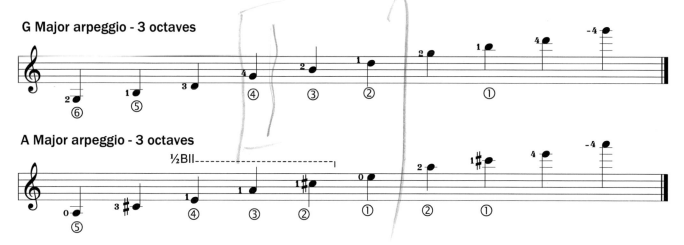

G Major arpeggio - 3 octaves

A Major arpeggio - 3 octaves

G Minor arpeggio - 3 octaves

A Minor arpeggio - 3 octaves

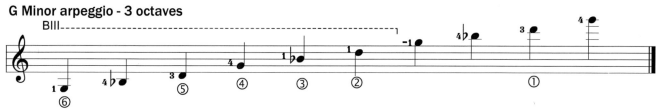
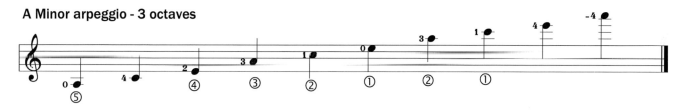

E Minor chord - 3 different fingerboard positions

7

Key Study

The examiner will request a selection of the scales below,
plus ONE melodic theme of the *candidate's choice.*

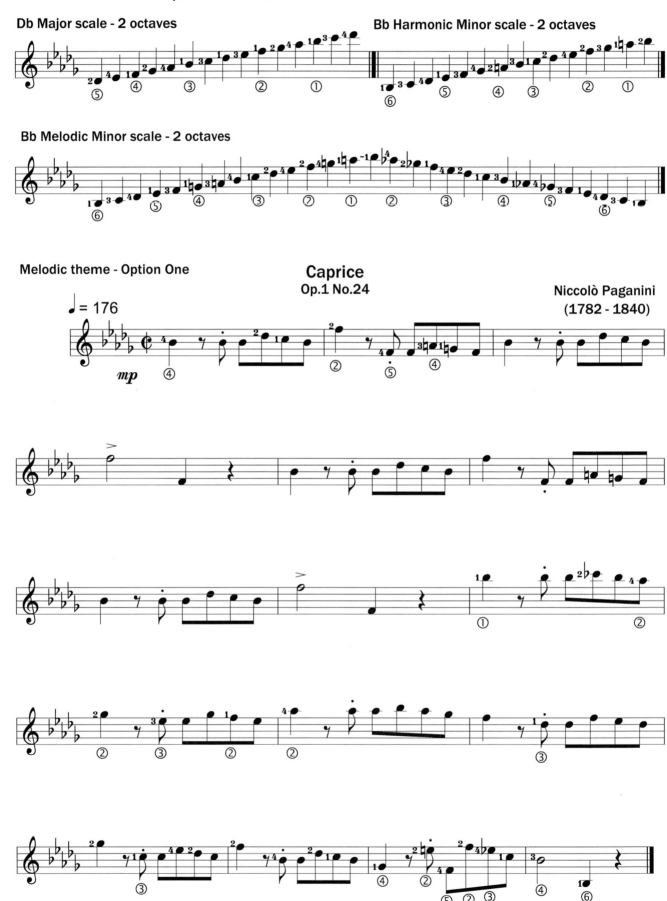

Db Major scale - 2 octaves

Bb Harmonic Minor scale - 2 octaves

Bb Melodic Minor scale - 2 octaves

Melodic theme - Option One

Caprice
Op.1 No.24

Niccolò Paganini
(1782 - 1840)

♩ = 176

mp

Melodic theme - Option Two

Salut D'Amour
Op.12

Edward Elgar
(1857 - 1934)

PERFORMANCE

Candidates should play *three* pieces. The programme should be balanced, with some contrasting pieces to demonstrate the candidate's range. At least two of the pieces must be chosen from those included in this handbook; the third piece can also be from the handbook *or*, if preferred, it can be either a 'free choice' piece of the candidate's own choosing – providing it is of at least a similar technical level to the pieces in this handbook – or it can be a piece taken from the supplementary list shown in the LCM Exams Repertoire List for this grade (viewable via the RGT website www.RegistryOfGuitarTutors.com or obtainable from LCM Exams).

Performance Tips

The performance notes below are intended to provide helpful advice and information, however candidates are free to present alternative technical solutions and musical interpretations – providing that a musically effective and stylistically appropriate result is achieved.

Melancholy Galliard *(Dowland)*:

John Dowland is undoubtedly the most renowned lutenist of all time. He lived in England, and travelled widely across Europe. He was appointed as Lutenist of the Royal Court in both Denmark and England. Dowland was also one of the most successful songwriters of his period. Although a *Galliard* is normally considered a fairly lively dance, the Melancholy title of this piece indicates a much slower and more tempered approach. The piece is in three distinct eight bar sections; each followed by a division, i.e. an elaborated variation.

Courante *(Praetorius)*:

This courante is taken from Praetorius' anthology *Terpsichore*, a collection of dances published in 1612, originally written in several staves for unspecified instruments, but usually performed by strings or recorders; it is arranged here for guitar by guitarist Neil Smith. A courante is a quick dance from the late Renaissance and Baroque periods. The main technical challenge is negotiating the many chords in the piece fluently. Be careful to project the moving middle part above the upper pedal notes in the section from bar 30 onwards.

Allemande *(J.S. Bach)*:

German composer Johann Sebastian Bach was best known during his lifetime as a highly respected organist. Today he is recognised worldwide as one of the foremost composers of all time, particularly for his skilled use of contrapuntal writing. This Allemande is the second movement from his *Lute Suite BWV996*, written in the first quarter of the 18th century. Attention should be given to the phrasing and voicing so as to realise the full effectiveness of the two-part contrapuntal writing.

Scherzando *(Coste)*:

Born in 1805, Coste was a student of Fernando Sor and went on to become one of France's most respected guitarists. He composed over 50 sets of works, almost entirely for guitar. This piece is from his collection *25 Etudes de Genre Op.38*, published in 1873 for the seven-string guitar which included an extended fingerboard. The title *Scherzando* suggests a playful and light-hearted approach should be taken. Be careful to observe all the rests, as they help define the phrasing.

Cantabile *(Sor)*:

Born in Spain, Fernando Sor also lived in England, Russia and France. He was a renowned guitarist and prolific composer, writing over 400 pieces for the guitar. This piece forms part of his collection *Six Bagatelles Opus 43*. The *cantabile* marking suggests that the piece should be played in 'a singing style' – emphasising the need for well-structured melodic phrasing. Be careful to observe all the crotchet rests that often mark the end of a two bar phrase. The harmonics in the final section will be easier to sound clearly if the right hand picks very close to the bridge. For ease of comparison between all the harmonics in this piece, they are written in this edition at the pitch of the open string on which they are played; the fret number being shown above each harmonic.

Allegro Brillante *(Carcassi)*:

Born in Italy, Matteo Carcassi later made France his home. As a virtuoso performer on the guitar, Carcassi regularly toured Europe. He wrote much music for the guitar, including many studies and a successful guitar teaching method. This is the final piece in his popular collection *25 Melodic And Progressive Studies Opus 60*. The piece is heavily chordal based so, wherever possible, left-hand fingers should be held on within bars to create a legato sound. In particular, the bass notes marked with tenuto lines should be held and slightly emphasised – as although the piece has been arranged here in a single line for clarity of reading, the writing clearly implies two voices.

Gran Vals *(Tárrega)*:

Spanish guitarist Francisco Tárrega is often called 'the father of the modern classical guitar' due to his great influence on expanding its technique and repertoire. This piece was first published in 1902. The numerous slide signs that appear in this piece should be observed as they form an integral part of the music and are typical in Tárrega's writing as a way of adding expression. Although rubato can be effectively employed in places, the waltz feel should be maintained. The accompaniment chords should be carefully contained so as not to overpower the melody.

Candombe En Mi *(M.D.Pujol)*:

The Argentinean composer Maximo Diego Pujol is not to be confused with the Spanish composer Emilio Pujol. *Candombe En Mi* is the last in a set of five preludes. A candombe is a lively, rhythmic music and dance style from Uruguay, although its roots are from Africa. Be sure to observe the many accented notes and chords occurring throughout the piece. The notation in this handbook version is taken directly from the publisher's manuscript edited by John W. Duarte; slurs are indicated by a series of dots forming a dotted curved line.

Melancholy Galliard

John Dowland
(1563 - 1626)

Courante

**Michael Praetorius
(1571 – 1621)**

♩. = 63

⑥ = D

Arranged by Neil Smith. From 'Six Dances' by M.Praetorius.

Allemande

Johann Sebastian Bach
(1685 - 1750)

Scherzando Op.38 No.8

**Napoléon Coste
(1805 – 1883)**

Cantabile Op.43 No.3

Fernando Sor
(1778 - 1839)

Allegro Brillante Op.60 No.25

[Group A]

Matteo Carcassi
(1792 - 1853)

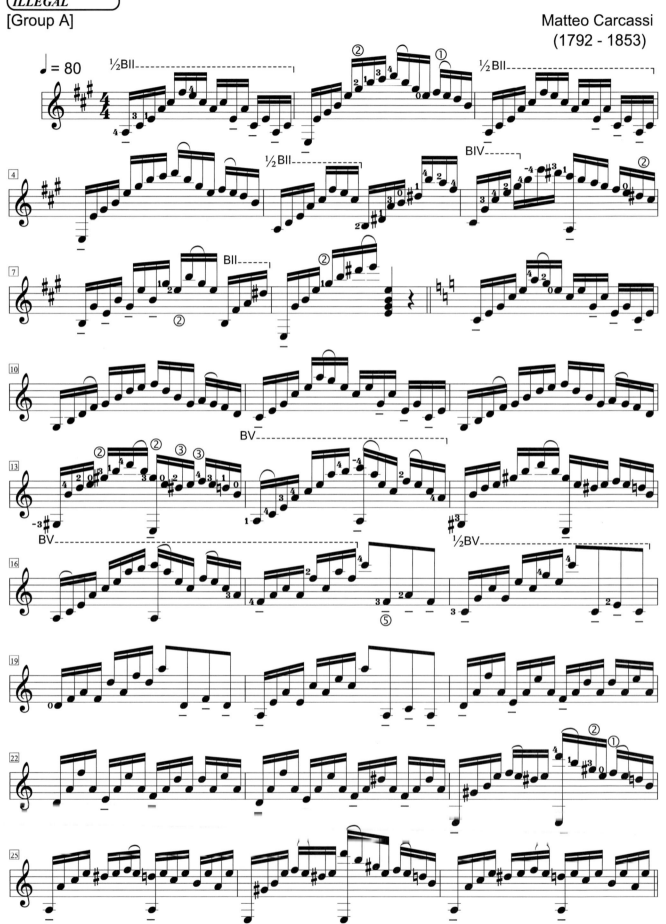

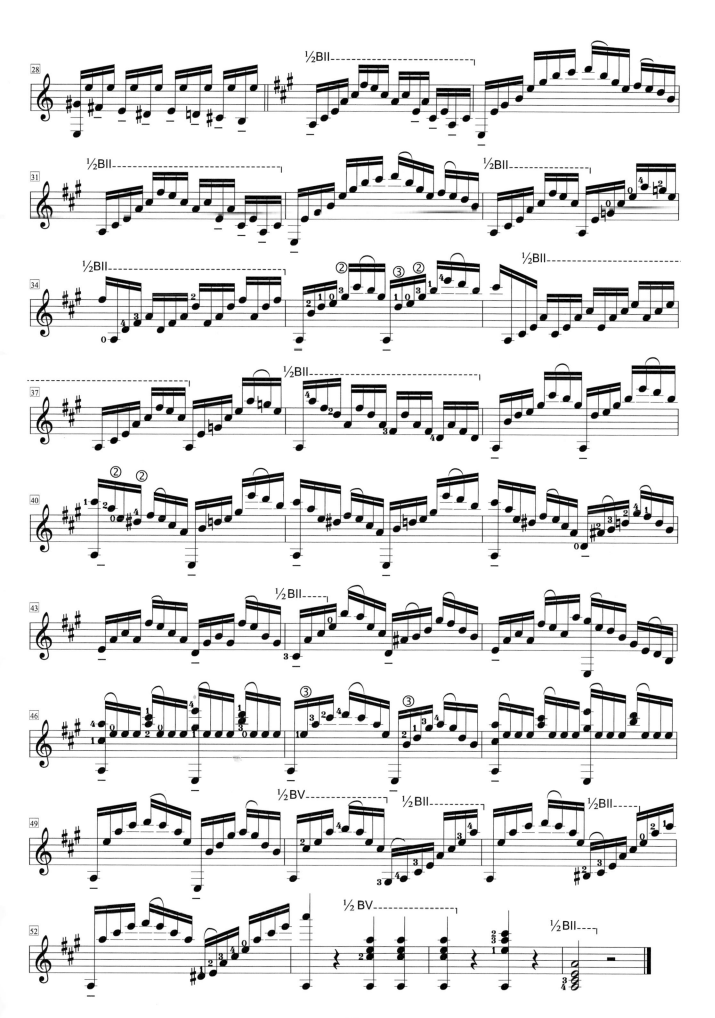

Gran Vals

Francisco Tárrega
(1852 - 1909)

Candombe En Mi

Máximo Diego Pujol
(1957 –)

♩ = 120

Tempo di candombe (Allegro ritmico)

✕ - *golpe* on belly of guitar

⊗ - *golpe* on bridge

VIVA VOCE_____

n this section of the examination candidates will be engaged in a short discussion to enable the examiner to assess the candidate's understanding of musical fundamentals and their responses to the pieces played. A maximum of 7 marks may be awarded.

At this grade candidates should be able to:

- explain the meaning of all notational elements in the music performed in the Performance component of the exam;

- identify intervals, cadences and chords occurring in the music;

- identify melodic and harmonic features of the music (e.g. modulations, sequence, melodic inversion, circle of 5ths, pedal points, etc.);

- demonstrate knowledge of formal structures (e.g. binary, ternary, etc.);

- provide basic biographical information about the composers of the music performed;

- demonstrate awareness of the historical and stylistic context of the music performed as well as a widening musical awareness extending a little beyond the music performed;

- demonstrate an understanding of the workings and anatomy of the guitar;

- describe the mood and character of pieces using appropriate descriptive terminology and identify contrasts of mood within pieces and describe any pictorial or descriptive element of the music;

- discuss their personal responses to the music performed, i.e. the extent to which they like or dislike it, or find it challenging or rewarding, and why;

- discuss their approaches to learning the pieces including the use of certain techniques, aspects of interpretation and identifying any particular difficulties (musical or technical) that were encountered;

- demonstrate a self-critical awareness of their own performance, indicating to the examiner which aspects of their performance they were happy or unhappy with, and why.

Potential candidates lacking knowledge in this general area are advised to study for the London College of Music Theory of Music examinations, using suitable music theory books, worksheets and musical dictionaries. Advice and tuition from an experienced teacher would undoubtedly prove most advantageous.

Below are some examples of the *type* of questions that the examiner may ask at this grade - although the overall number of questions will not be as extensive as all the examples given below. Note that these are examples only; the list is by no means exhaustive. The wording and phrasing of the questions may vary even when the same topic is involved. The examiner's questions will be limited to one or more of the pieces performed.

Specimen answers are provided below based on J.S. Bach's *Allemande* in order to give some indication of the depth and detail required in responses; it is stressed that these answers are samples and by no means definitive. Specimen answers are deliberately not supplied for other pieces in order to encourage candidates to undertake broader research and to avoid the temptation to learn answers by rote.

Allemande *(Bach)*

Question: What can you tell me about J.S. Bach?

Answer: German composer Johann Sebastian Bach was best known during his lifetime as a highly respected organist. He lived between 1685 and 1750, i.e. towards the end of the Baroque period. Today he is recognised worldwide as one of the foremost composers of all time, particularly for his skilled use of fugue and counterpoint.

Question: Describe the form and main key changes of this piece.

Answer: The piece is in Binary Form - so it is in two sections. The first section begins in E minor and ends in the dominant, B major, after 8 bars. The second section begins briefly in B, but then modulates through a variety of key centres before ending in E major.

Question: What can you tell me about the style and origin of the Allemande?

Answer: The Allemande is a dance, of German origin, of moderate tempo in quadruple time. It is in Binary Form and, as in this piece, each section normally begins with a short upbeat note.

Question: Tell me about the historical context of this Allemande.

Answer: The Allemande was a standard component, normally being the first or second movement, of the Baroque suite - an instrumental composition consisting of a chain of stylised dance forms. In this instance, the Allemande is the second movement from Bach's Lute Suite BWV996.

Gran Vals *(Tárrega)*

Question: Identify the principal modulations that occur within this piece.

Question: Can you describe the chord that is formed by the notes in bar 12?

Question: Identify the interval between the two notes (D and G#) that occur on the last beat of bar 30.

Question: Explain the meaning of terms *ritard* and *a piacere* (that appear under bars 44 and 45).

Question: What type of cadence is created between the final chord in bar 46 and the chord in bar 47?

Melancholy Galliard *(Dowland)*

Question: Describe the structure of this piece.

Question: Describe some of the prominent rhythmic, melodic or harmonic features of the piece.

Question: What was the most difficult thing about learning this piece?

Question: How do you feel your performance of this piece went today?

Question: Can you provide some basic biographical information about John Dowland?

SIGHT READING

The examiner will show you the sight reading test and allow you just a short time to look over it before performing it. The piece will be 8 bars long, and may contain 4 note chords, triplets and syncopated rhythms. The key signature range will be 3 flats to 4 sharps. The fingerboard range will not exceed 7th position. The time signature will be either $\frac{2}{4}$, $\frac{3}{4}$, $\frac{4}{4}$, $\frac{2}{2}$ or $\frac{6}{8}$. Up to 10 marks may be awarded.

The examples below show the type of pieces that will be presented in the examination.

AURAL TESTS

A maximum of 8 marks may be awarded in this section of the examination: up to 2 marks for Test 1a, up to 4 marks for Test 1b and up to 2 marks for Test 2.

Test 1

A harmonised passage of approximately 12 to 16 bars in length, in either simple or compound time, will be played, once. Candidates will be asked a selection of the following:

- to identify the time signature
- to identify whether the passage is in a major or minor key
- to describe the overall dynamics
- to describe the basic overall form (this will be limited to AB, ABA, AAB, ABAB, AABA)

Test 1b

The candidate will be given a copy of the score, *with all phrasing, tempo, articulation and dynamic markings omitted*. The passage will be played once again in full; further shorter sections may also be played again. Candidates will be asked a selection of the following:

- to suggest an appropriate tempo marking
- to describe changes in tempo
- to name the key
- to describe phrasing patterns
- to describe dynamics

- to describe articulation
- to identify modulations
- to identify ornaments
- to confirm their description of the form

The tests will be played by the examiner on either piano or guitar, at the examiner's discretion. The examples below provide a broad indication of the *type* of tests that may be given during the examination.

So that candidates are prepared for viewing the score in piano notation during the examination, sample tests are also provided in piano notation. (It should be noted that these are *not* direct transcriptions of the sample guitar tests.)

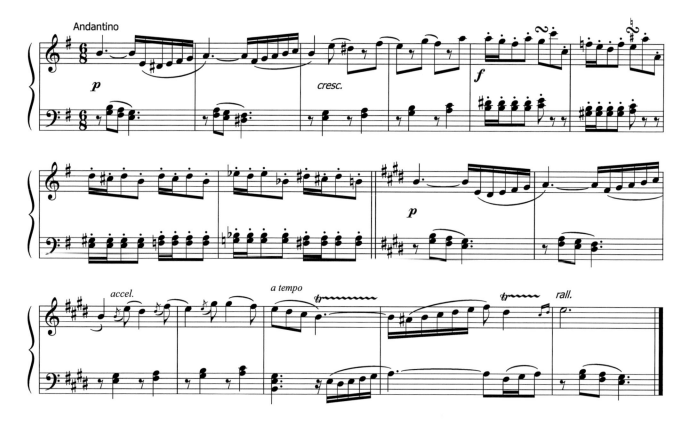

Test 2

The candidate will be asked to identify two of the four common cadences in either major or minor keys. Each will be played as a separate example, preceded by a short harmonised 'lead-in' with the cadence forming the last two chords. Here are some examples.

Perfect

Perfect

Plagal

Imperfect

Interrupted

LONDON COLLEGE OF MUSIC

Classical Guitar
Examination Entry Form
GRADE SEVEN
or Leisure Play Advanced

The standard LCM Exams music entry form is NOT valid for Classical Guitar entries.
Entry to the examination is only possible via this original form.
Photocopies of this form will not be accepted under any circumstances.

Please use black ink and block capital letters when completing this form.

Circle the type of examination you wish to enter: • Grade examination   • Leisure Play examination.

SESSION (Spring/Summer/Winter): _____ YEAR: _____

Preferred Examination Centre (if known): _____
If left blank you will be examined at the nearest venue to your home address.

Candidate Details:

Candidate Name (as to appear on certificate):

_____

Candidate ID (if entered previously): _____ Date of birth: _____

Gender (M/F): _____ Ethnicity (see chart overleaf): _____

Date of birth and ethnicity details are for statistical purposes only, and are not passed on to the examiner.

☐ Tick this box if you are attaching details of particular needs requirements.

Teacher Details:

Teacher Name (as to appear on certificate): _____

Teacher Qualifications (if required on certificate): _____

LCM Teacher Code (if entered previously): _____

Address: _____

_____ Postcode: _____

Tel. No. (day): _____ (evening): _____

☐ Tick this box if any details above have changed since your last LCM entry.

IMPORTANT NOTES

- It is the candidate's responsibility to have knowledge of, and comply with, the current syllabus requirements. Where candidates are entered for examinations by a teacher, the teacher must take responsibility that candidates are entered in accordance with the current syllabus requirements. Failure to carry out any of the examination requirements may lead to disqualification.

- For candidates with particular needs, a letter giving details and requests for any special requirements (e.g. enlarged sight reading), together with an official supporting document (e.g. medical certificate), should be attached.

- Examinations may be held on any day of the week, including weekends. Any appointment requests (e.g. 'prefer morning,' or 'prefer weekdays') must be made at the time of entry. **LCM Exams and its Representatives will take note of the information given; however, no guarantees can be made that all wishes can be met.**

- Submission of this entry is an undertaking to abide by the current regulations.

ETHNIC ORIGIN CLASSIFICATIONS

White
01   British
02   Irish
03   Other white background

Mixed
04   White and black Caribbean
05   White and black African
06   White and Asian
07   Other mixed background

Asian or Asian British
08   Indian
09   Pakistani
10   Bangladeshi
11   Other Asian background

Black or Black British
12   Caribbean
13   African
14   Other black background

Chinese or Other Ethnic Group
15   Chinese
16   Other

17   **Prefer not to say**

Examination Fee: £ _____

Late Entry Fee (if necessary)   £ _____

Total amount submitted: £ _____

Cheques or postal orders should be made payable to '*Thames Valley University*'.

A list of current fees, entry deadlines and session dates is available from LCM Exams.

Where to submit your entry form

Entries for public centres should be sent to the
**LCM Exams local examination centre representative
(NOT to the LCM Exams Head Office).**

View the LCM Exams website   http://mercury.tvu.ac.uk/lcmexams
or contact the LCM Exams office (tel: 020 8231 2364 / email: lcm.exams@tvu.ac.uk)
for details of your nearest local examination centre representative.

Entries for the London area only, or for private centres, should be sent direct to:
LCM Exams, Thames Valley University, Walpole House, 10-22 Bond St, London, W5 5AA

Official Entry Form